BBC

Ludwig

THE BEATLES

Selections from
The Beatles
'Live at the BBC'

ISBN 0-7935-6206-6

7777 W. BLUEMOUND RD. P.O. BOX 13819 MILWAUKEE, WI 53213

Photographs by Dezo Hoffmann
Photographs reproduced by kind permission of Apple Corps Ltd.
Book design by Studio Twenty, London

Printed in the United Kingdom by
J.B. Offset Printers (Marks Tey) Limited, Marks Tey, Essex.

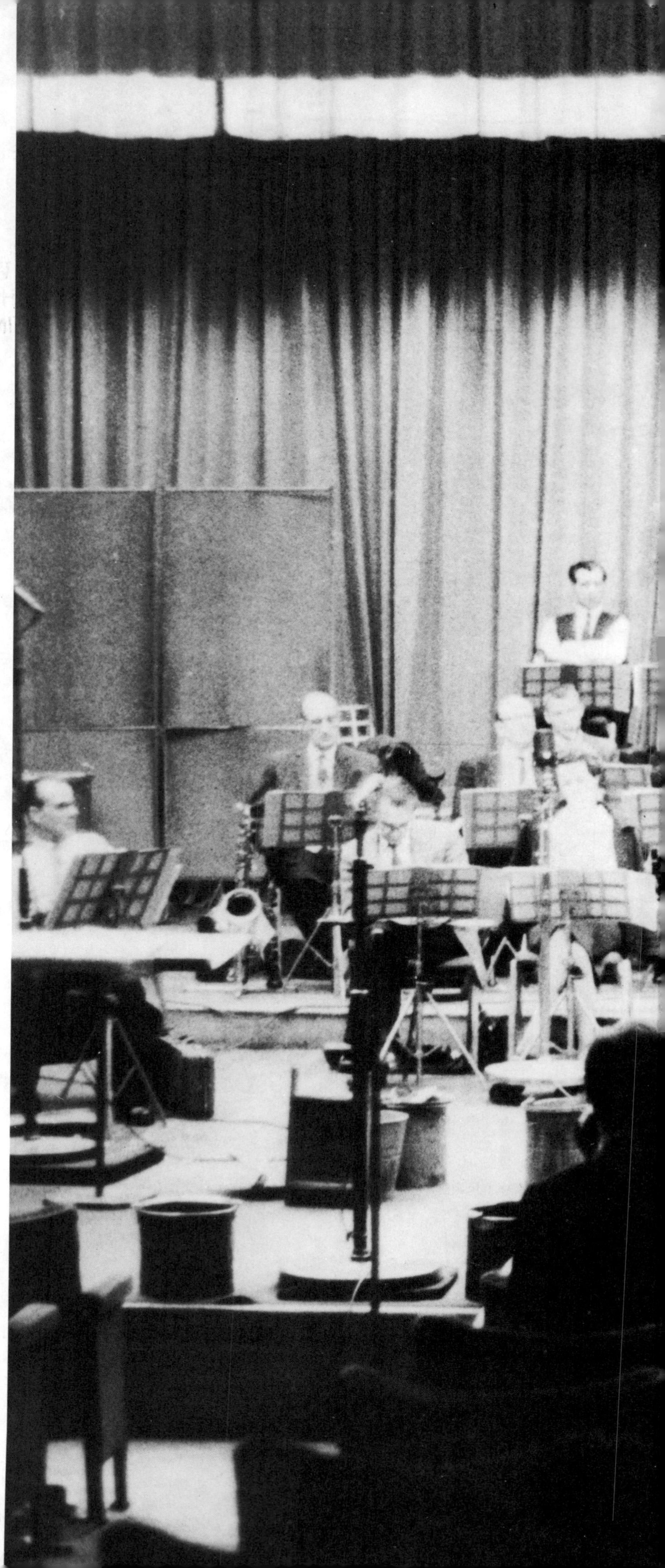

VOX

BRITISH
RAILWAYS
travel centre
BEA

I'll Be On My Way
Page 6
Thank You Girl
Page 8
You Really Got A Hold On Me
Page 14
To Know Her Is To Love Her
Page 11
A Taste Of Honey
Page 18
Long Tall Sally
Page 22
I Saw Her Standing There
Page 25
Can't Buy Me Love
Page 30
Till There Was You
Page 33
A Hard Day's Night
Page 36
I Wanna Be Your Man
Page 44
Roll Over Beethoven
Page 41
All My Loving
Page 48
Things We Said Today
Page 56
She's A Woman
Page 51
I Feel Fine
Page 60
I'm A Loser
Page 70
Everybody's Trying To Be My Baby
Page 64
Rock And Roll Music
Page 76
Ticket To Ride
Page 78
Dizzy Miss Lizzy
Page 73
Kansas City/Hey! Hey! Hey! Hey!
Page 90
Matchbox
Page 82
Honey Don't
Page 86
Love Me Do
Page 93

I'll Be on My Way

Words and Music by John Lennon and Paul McCartney

♩ = 126

A Aaug A6 Aaug

mf

1. The

A E A D

sun is fad - ing a - way, That's the end __ of the day,
2.3. They were right, __ I was wrong; True love did - n't last long,

A E7 A D To Coda A

As the June ___ light turns to moon - light, I'll be on my way.

E A D

Just one kiss, __ then I'll go, Don't hide the tears __ that don't show.

(2° instr.)

A
E7
A
D
As the June light turns to moon - light, I'll be on my
A
B7
E
B7
way. To where the winds don't blow, and gold - en riv - ers
(vocal 2°)
E
F♯7
B7
E7
D.S. al Coda
flow, This way will I go.
Coda
A
E
A
A aug
A6
A aug
Repeat and Fade
way. I'll be on my way, oh.

Thank You Girl

Words and Music by John Lennon and Paul McCartney

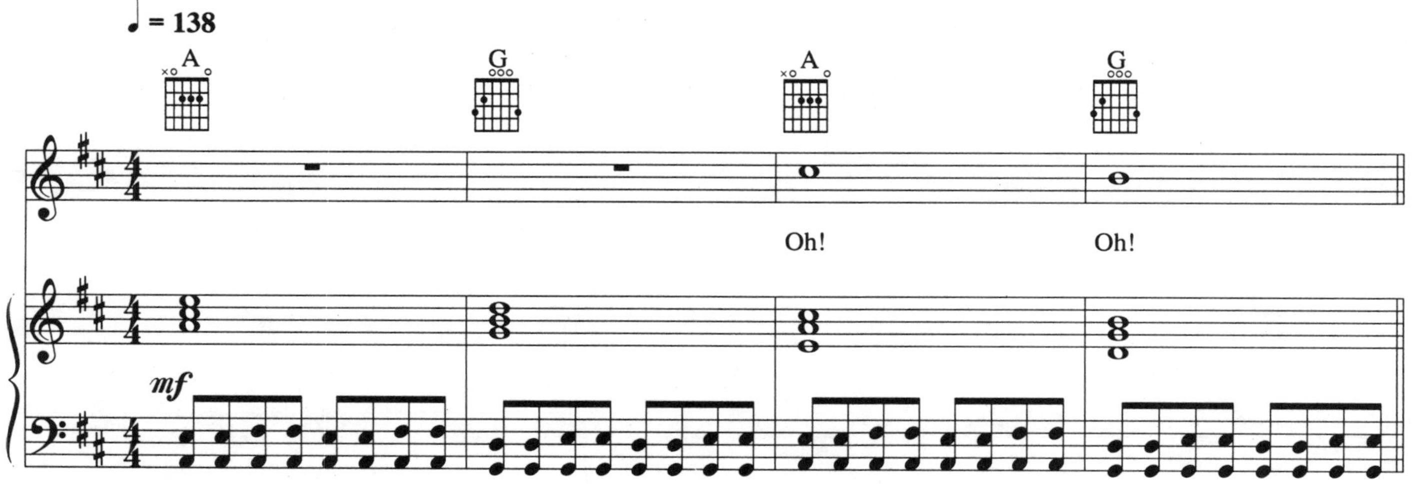

D
A
D
G
be in love with you.
fool would doubt our love.
And all I got - ta
A
G
To Coda
1. A
do is thank you, girl;
thank you, girl.
2. A
Bm
D
A7
thank you, girl.
Thank you, girl, for lov - in' me the way that you do.
Em
A
D
(way that you do)
That's the kind of love that is too good to be true.

G
A
G
And all I got - ta do is thank you, girl;
A
D.C. al Coda
thank you, girl.
Coda
A
thank you, girl.
G
A
G
D
G
Oh!
Oh!
Oh!
D
G
A
G
D
D6
Oh!
Oh!

To Know Her Is to Love Her

Words and Music by Phil Spector

♩. = 68

E B

1, 3. To know know know– her, – is to love love love– her, –

(Verse 2 see block lyric)

C♯m A

just to see her smile– makes my life worth-while, – just to

E B E A

know know know– her, – is to love love love– her, – and I do, and I do and I

1. E B7

do.

2, 3. E

do

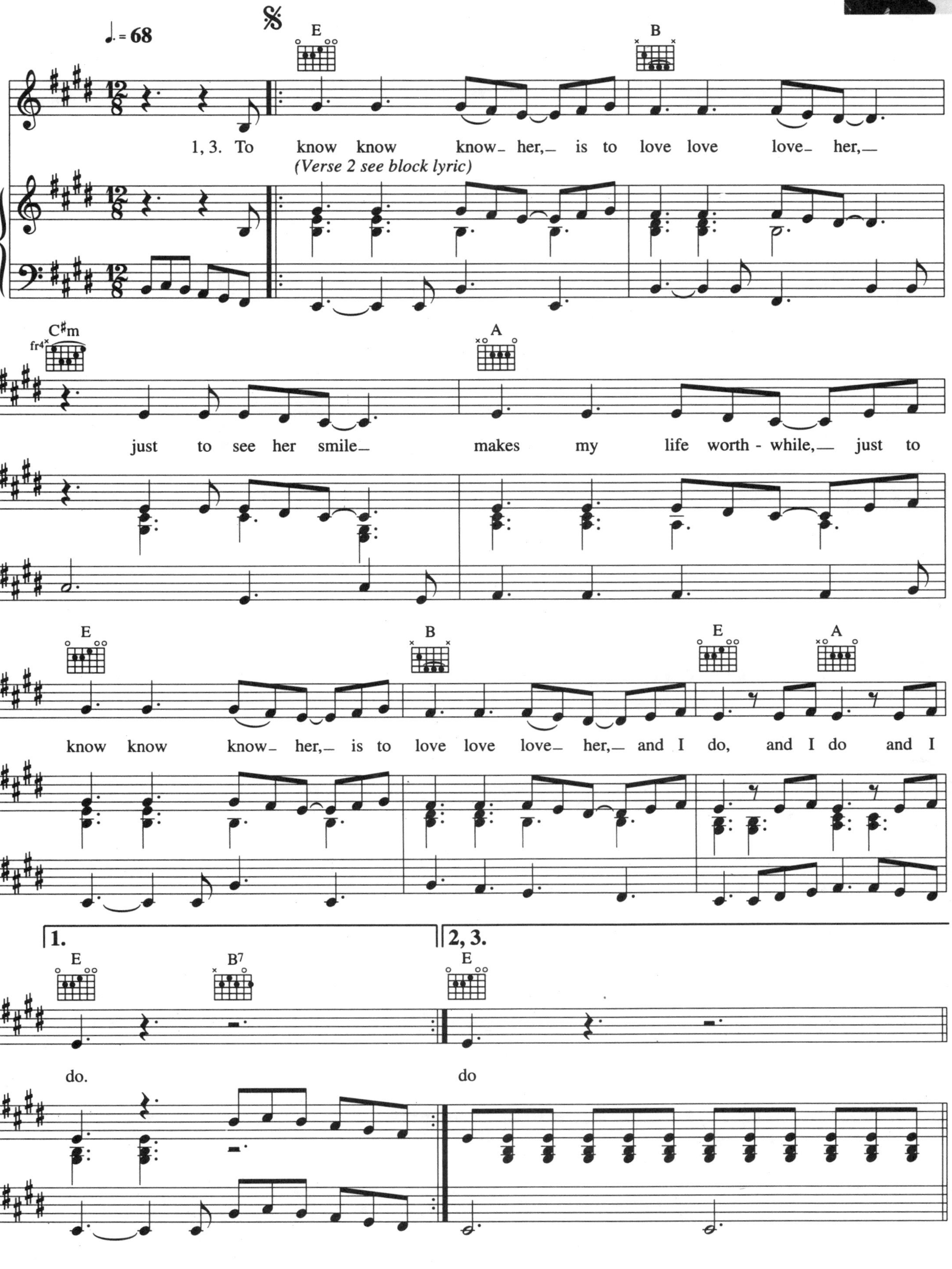

G
D
C
Why can't you see, how blind can she
B7
G
E
C–
B7
be? Some - day she'll see that
F♯
B7
D.%. al Coda
To Coda ⊕
she was meant just for me. To
⊕ Coda
E
B
know know know her, is to love love love her,

Verse 2:
I'll be good to her,
I'll make love to her
Everyone says there'll come a day
When I'll walk alongside of her
Yes just to know know know her
Is to love love love her
And I do and I do
And I do.

You Really Got a Hold on Me

Words and Music by William "Smokey" Robinson

♩. = 82

A F♯m

A

1. I don't like you, but I love you;
2. I don't want you, but I need you;
3. I wan - na leave you, don't wan - na stay here;

F♯m

seems that I'm al - ways think - ing of you.
don't wan - na kiss you, but I need to.
don't wan - na spend an - oth - er day here.

A D

oh, oh, oh, you treat me bad - ly, I love you
oh. oh, oh, you do me wrong now, my love is
oh, oh, oh, I wan - na split now, I just can't

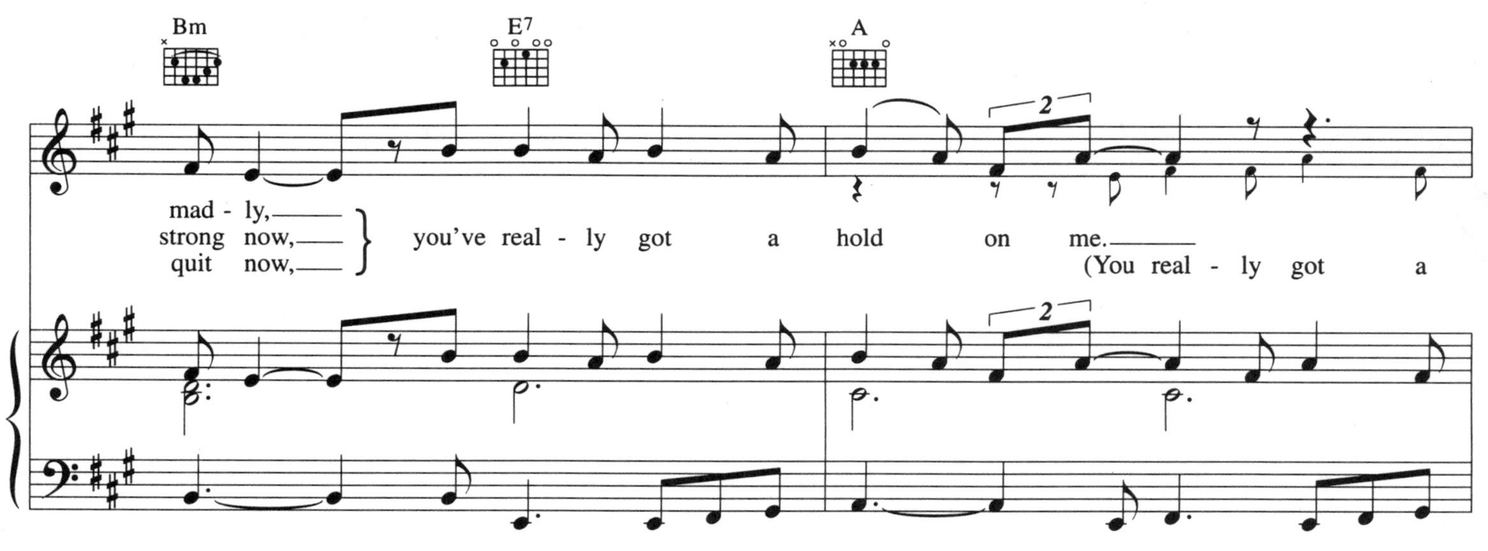
Bm
E7
A
mad - ly,
strong now,
quit now,
you've real - ly got a hold on me.
(You real - ly got a

1.
F♯m
You real - ly got a hold on me.
hold on me.)
(You real - ly got a

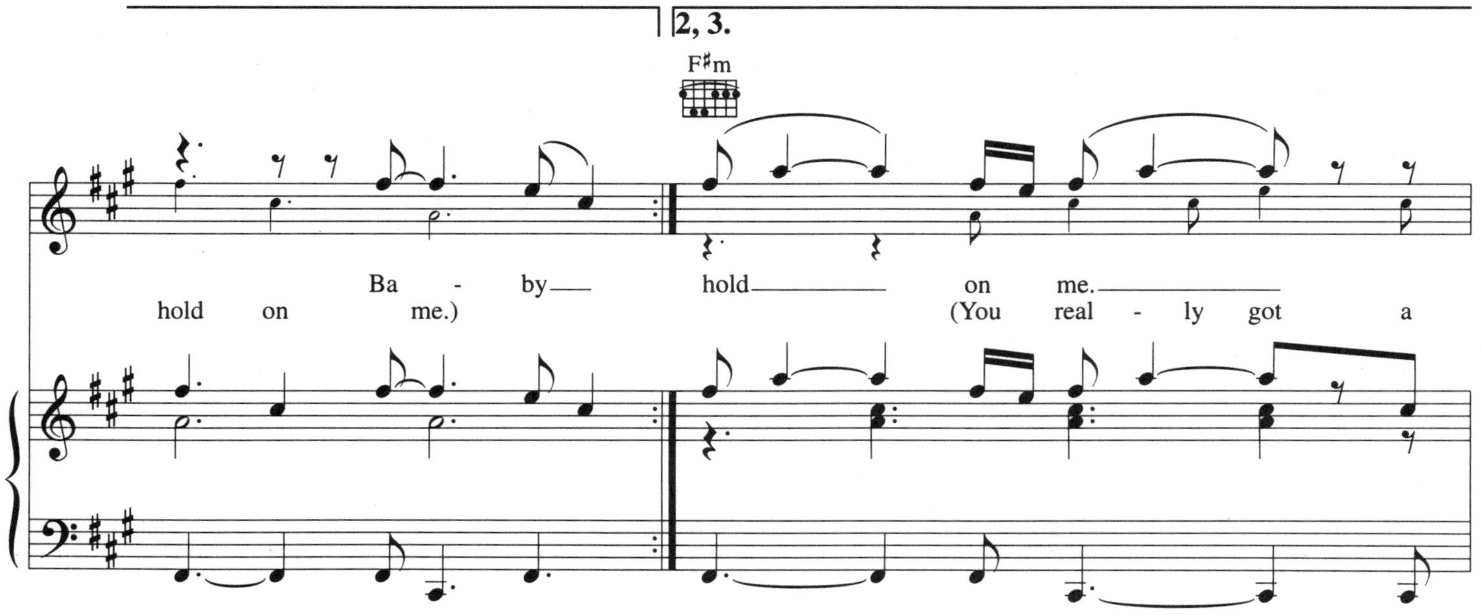
2, 3.
F♯m
Ba - by hold on me.
hold on me.)
(You real - ly got a

A
A7
Ba - by, I love you and all I
hold on me.)
D
A
want you to do is just (1.) hold me, hold me,
(2.) hold me, (please) hold me, (squeeze)
E7
To Coda
a tempo
hold me, hold me.
hold me, hold me.
A
F♯m
E
A
Tight - er!

F♯m
E
A
D.𝄋. al Coda
Tight - er!
𝄌 Coda
A
You real - ly got a hold on me.
(You real - ly got a hold on me.)
F♯m
You real - ly got a hold on me.
(You real - ly got a hold on me.)
A
A9
fr6

A Taste of Honey

Words and Music by Ric Marlow and Bobby Scott

Freely and slowly

F♯m A E

(Choir) A taste of hon - ey, *(Solo)* tast - ing much sweet - er than

Moderately
♩= 100

F♯m

wine. *(Choir)* (doo dood - n' doo) (doo dood - n' doo) *(Solo)* 1. I

𝄋

F♯m F♯m(maj7) fr4 F♯m7 B

dream of your first kiss and then, I
was the kiss that a - woke my heart. There

F♯m
F♯m(maj7)
fr4
B
feel up - on my lips a - gain, a taste of
lin - gers still, though we're far a - part, that taste of
A
(Choir)
(Solo)
hon - ey. (A taste of hon - ey.) Tast - ing much
hon - ey. (A taste of hon - ey.)
E
Bm
sweet - er than wine.
Shuffle ♩=106
I will re - turn yes I
3

F♯m
B
To Coda
A
E
will re - turn, I'll come back for the hon - ey and
Tempo 1
F♯m
D.%. al Coda
you. (Doo doo - 'n doo, doo doo - 'n doo.) 2. Yours
Slower
A
Coda
(Choir)
E
(Solo)
back (He'll come back) for hon - ey (for the hon - ey) and
A tempo
F♯m
Bm
F♯m
Bm
F♯m
Bm
F♯
you.

Long Tall Sally

Words and Music by Enotris Johnson, Richard Penniman and Robert Blackwell

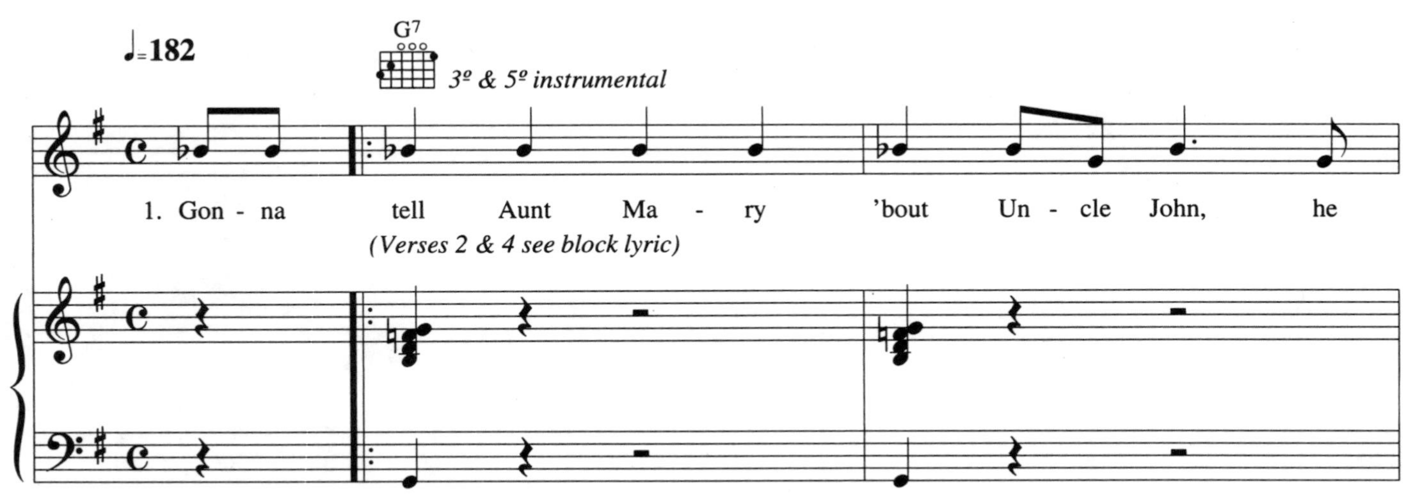

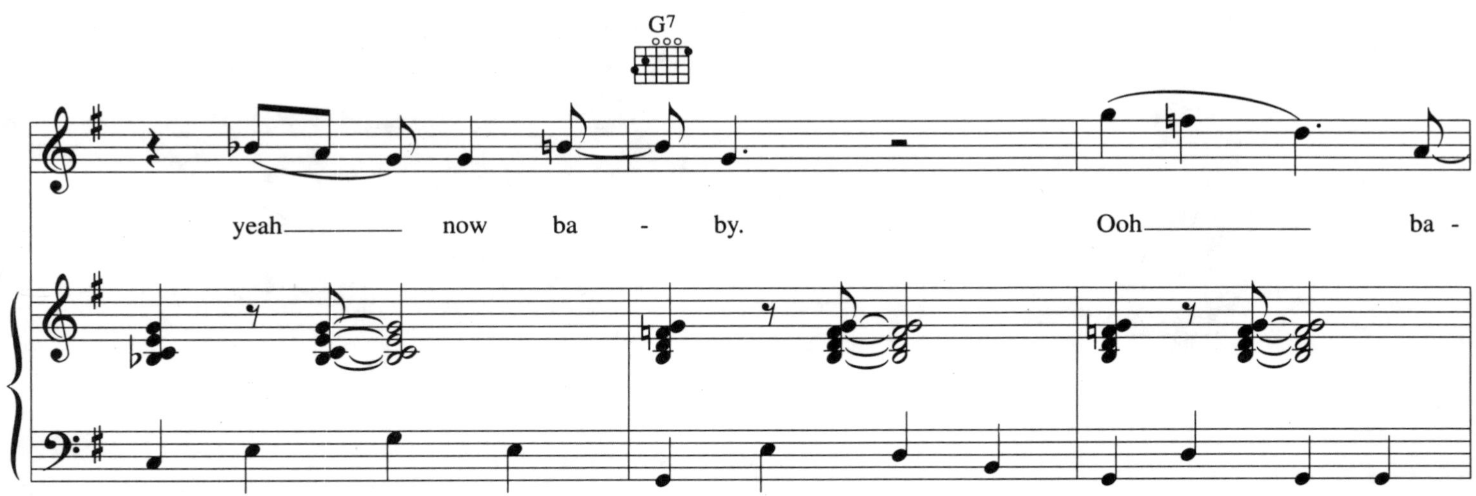

D7
C7
G
by,
some fun to - night.
1, 2, 3, 4.
5.
D7
D7
G7
Well I
Well, we're gon - na
have some fun to - night,
we're gon - na
have some fun to - night,
C7
G7
ev - 'ry - thing's all right,
yeah we'll have some fun to - night,

Verse 2:
Well I saw Uncle John with Long Tall Sally
He saw Aunt Mary coming so he ducked back in the alley
Oh baby
Yeah now baby
Ooh, baby
Having some fun tonight.

Verse 3: Instrumental

Verse 4:
Long Tall Sally's built pretty sweet
She got everything that Uncle John need
Oh baby
Yeah now baby
Ooh, baby
Having some fun tonight.

Verse 5: Instrumental

I Saw Her Standing There

Words and Music by John Lennon and Paul McCartney

E
E7
A
C
how could I dance with an - oth - er, woo,
She would - n't dance with an - oth - er, woo,
Since I

E
E7
B7
E7
1.
saw her stand - ing there.
2. Well, she

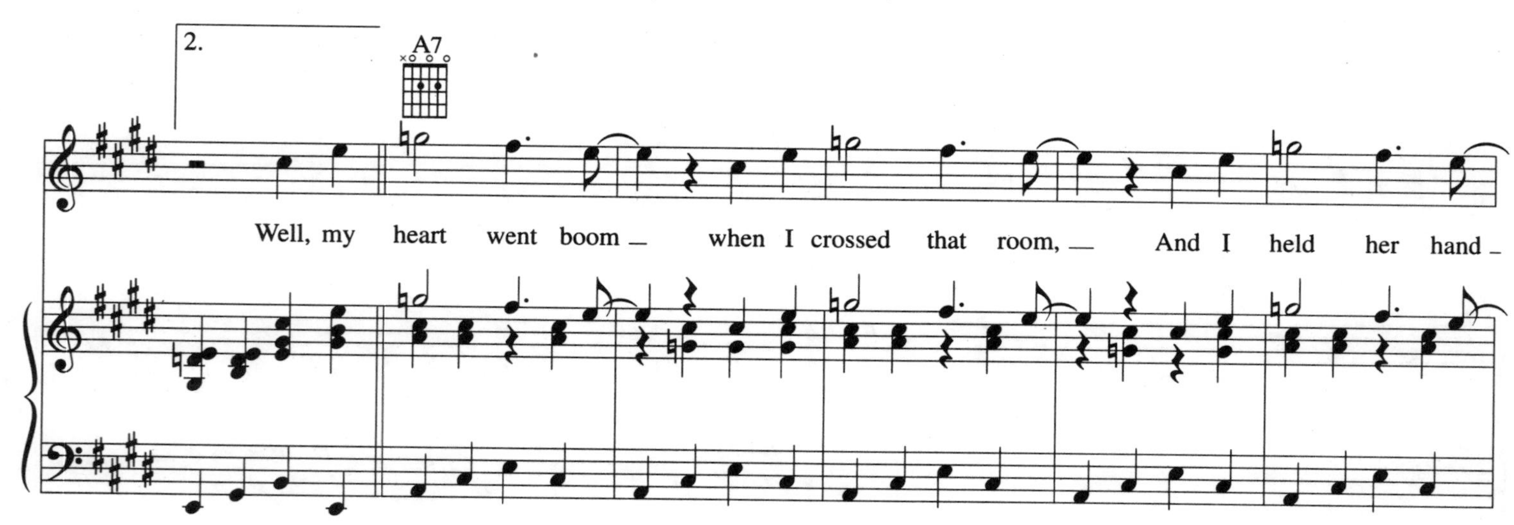
2.
A7
Well, my heart went boom when I crossed that room, And I held her hand

B7
A7
in mi - ne.
Oh, we danced
E7
A7
E7
through the night
and we held each oth - er tight,
And be -
B7
fore too long
I fell in love with her.
Now
E
E7
A
C
I'll nev - er dance
with an - oth - er, oh,
Since I

E
E7
B7
To Coda
E7
B7
saw her stand - ing there.
E7
B7
E7
A7

E7
B7
E7
B7
D.S. al Coda
Well we danced
Coda
E7
B7
Oh, since I saw her stand - ing there.
E7
E
E7
Yeah, well since I saw her
B7
A
E
E7
stand - ing there.

Can't Buy Me Love

Words and Music by John Lennon and Paul McCartney

♩ = 175

Em Am Em

Can't buy me love, oh, love, oh,

f

Am Dm7 G13 C

can't buy me love, oh. 1. I'll buy you a dia-mond ring,
2. give you all I've got
3. *Instrumental*

F7

my friend if it makes you feel all right, I'll get you an-y-thing,
to give if you say you love me too, I may not have a lot

C G

my friend, if it makes you feel al-right 'Cause / For } I don't care too
to give, But what I've got I'll give to you,

F7
Tacet
F7
1. C
2,3. C
much for mon - ey, for mon - ey can't buy me love. ___ 2. I'll ___ Can't buy me love, _
vocal 3x
Em
Am
C
___ oh, ev - 'ry - bod - y tells me so. ___ Can't buy me love, _
Em
Am
Dm7
G
C
___ oh, no no no ___ no! Say you don't need no dia -
F7
- mond rings _ and I'll be sat - is - fied, ___ Tell me that you want the kind _

C
G
of things that mon - ey just can't buy.
I don't care too
F7
To Coda
F7
C
Tacet
D.S. al Coda
much for mon - ey, mon - ey can't buy me love.
Coda
F7
C
Em
Am
mon - ey can't buy me love. Can't buy me love
love
Em
Am
Dm7
G13
C
can't buy me love.

Till There Was You

from Meredith Willson's THE MUSIC MAN

By Meredith Willson

B♭
B♭m
F
D7
D7(♭9)
mu - sic and won - der - ful ro - ses, they tell me, in
Gm7
G7
C7
C aug
C7
sweet. fra - grant mea - dows of dawn and dew. There was
F
F♯dim
Gm7
B♭m
love all a - round but I ne - ver heard it sing - ing, no, I
F
F/A
A♭m6
Gm7
C7
F
Gm7
C7
To Coda
ne - ver heard it at all, till there was you.
Solo

F
F♯dim
Gm7
B♭m
D.𝄋. al Coda
F
Am7
A♭m7
Gm7
G♭7(♯9)
F
C dim
F7
Then there was
⊕ Coda
C7
B
C7
Till
there was
F
D♭7
F
Fmaj7
you.

A Hard Day's Night

Words and Music by John Lennon and Paul McCartney

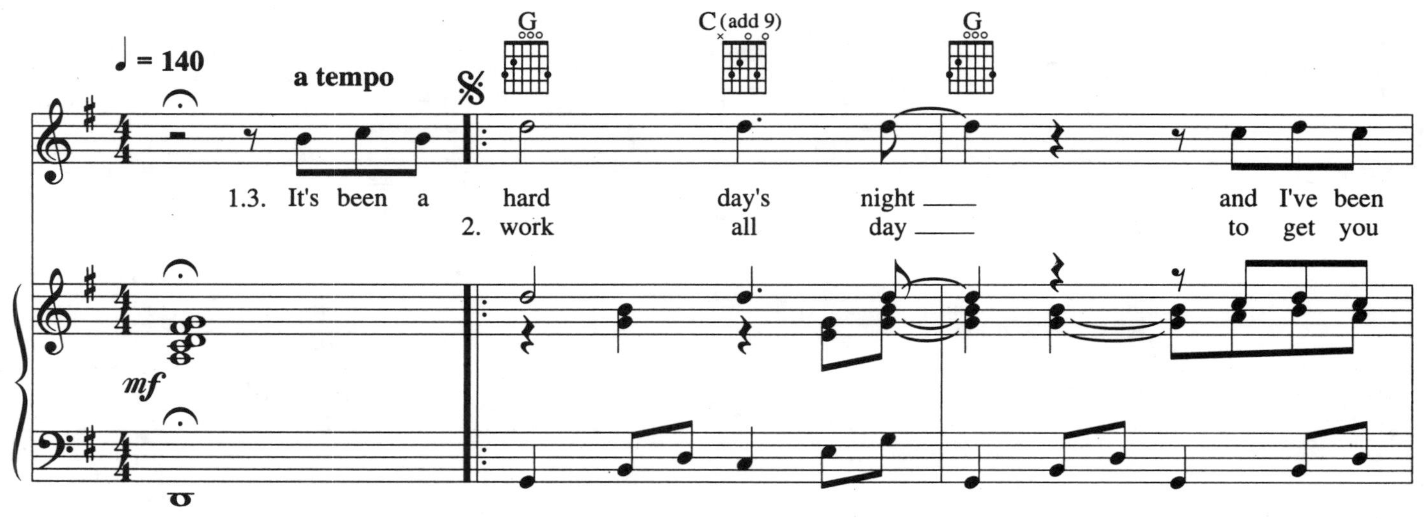

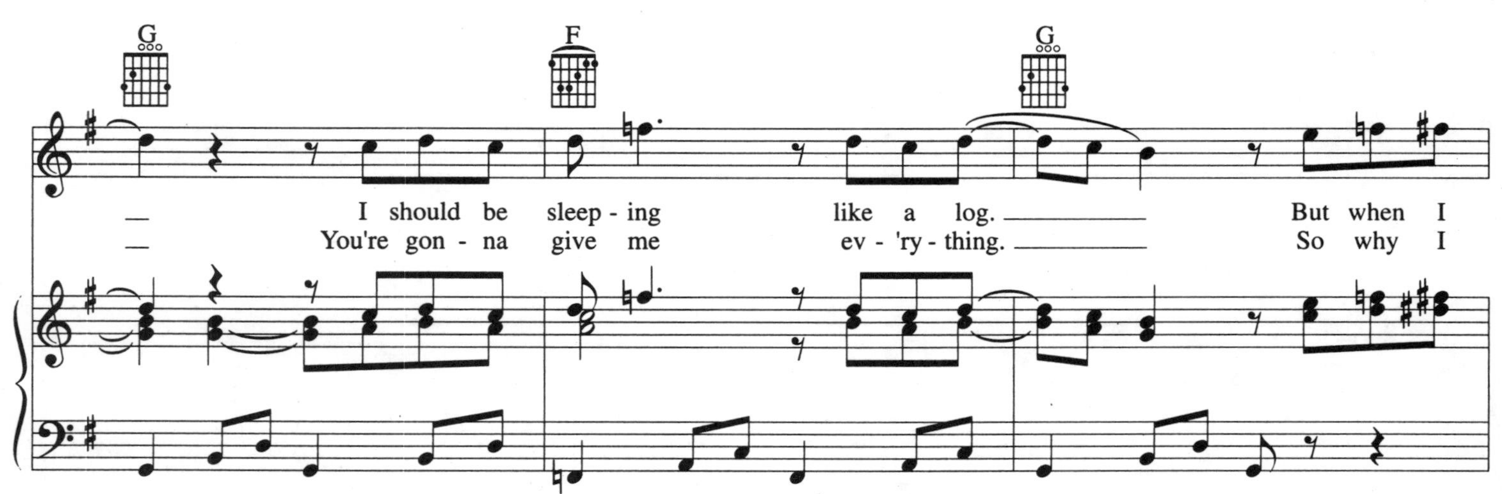

C
D
get home to you, I find the thing that you do will make me
love to come home 'Cause when I get you a - lone you know I'll
G
C9
To Coda
1.G
2. G
feel al - right. (2) You know I When I'm home
Bm
Em
Bm
ev - 'ry - thing seems to be right. When I'm home
G
Em
C
feel - ing you hold - ing me tight,

D
G
C (add 9)
G
tight, yeah. It's been a hard day's night and I've been
F
G
C (add 9)
work - ing like a dog. It's been a hard day's night
G
F
G
I should be sleep - ing like a log. But when I
C
D
G
C9
get home to you, I find the thing that you do will make me feel al - right.

G
D
G
C7
G
F
G
C7
G
F
G
C
D
So why I love to come home 'Cause when I get you a - lone you know I
G
C9
G
Bm
Em
feel al - right When I'm home ev - 'ry - thing seems to be

Bm
G
Em
right.
When I'm home
feel - ing you hold - ing me
C
D
D.S. al Coda
tight,
tight, yeah. It's been a
Coda
G
you know I
C9
G
C (add 9)
feel al - right,
you know I feel al - right.
F (add 9)
Repeat and Fade

Roll Over Beethoven

Words and Music by Chuck Berry

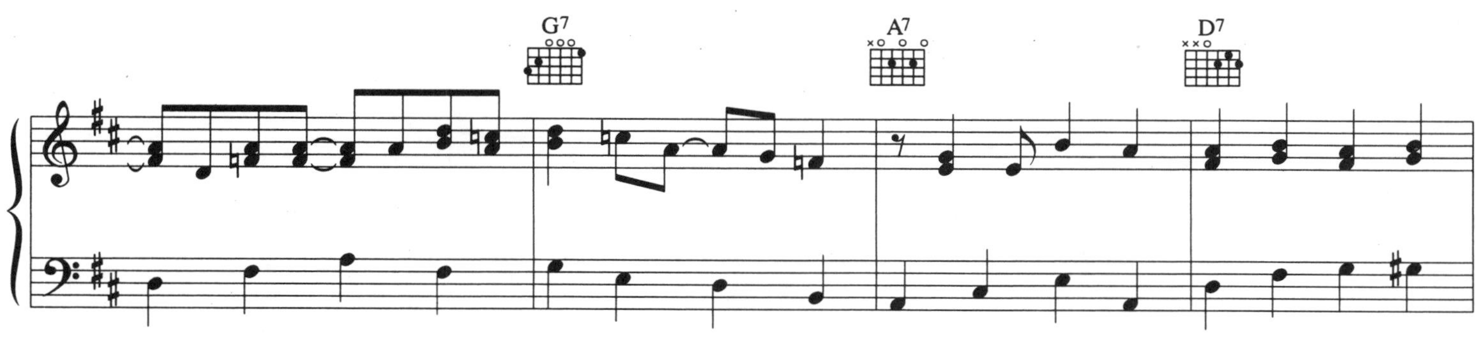

D7
G7
It's a rock-in' lit-tle re-cord I want my jock - ey to play.
D7
G7
A7
Roll ov - er Beet-ho - ven got-ta hear it a-gain to-day.
D7
1, 4.
2, 3, 5.
6.
2. You know my
5. Ear -
3. Well if you
6. You know she
Roll ov - er Beet -
D7
ho - ven, roll ov - er Beet - ho - ven, roll ov - er Beet -

Verse 2:
You know my temperature's rising, juke-box blows a fuse
My heart beatin' rhythm and my soul is a-singing the blues
Roll over Beehoven and tell Tchaikovsky the news.

Verse 3:
Well if you feel you like it, get your lover and reel and rock it, roll it over
Then move on up just a trifle further, then reel and rock it, roll it over
Roll over Beethoven, dig these rhythm and blues.

Verse 4: Instrumental

Verse 5:
Early in the morning I'm givin' you the warning, don't you step on my blue suede shoes
Hey diddle diddle, I'm a' playin' my fiddle, ain't got nothing to lose
Roll over Beethoven, we're rockin' it two by two.

Verse 6:
You know she wriggles like a glow-worm and dance like a spinning top
She's got a crazy partner, you ought to see them reel and rock
Long as she's got a dime the music will never stop.

I Wanna Be Your Man

Words and Music by John Lennon and Paul McCartney

𝅗𝅥 = 98

E7

𝄋 E7

1.3. I wan - na be your lov - er, ba - by, I wan - na be your man. __
2. Tell me that you love me, ba - by, Let me un - der - stand. __

__ I wan - na be your lov - er, ba - by,
__ Tell me that you love me, ba - by,

B7 E7

I wan - na be your man. ____ 1. Love you like no
I wan - na be your man. ____ 2.3. I wan - na be your

oth - er, ba - by, Like no oth - er can.
lov - er, ba - by, I wan - na be your man.
B7
Love you like no oth - er, ba - by, Like no oth - er can.
I wan - na be your lov - er, ba - by, I wan - na be your man.
E7
N.C.
F♯7
I wan - na be your man,
B7
E
C♯7
I wan - na be your man,
I wan - na be your man,

F♯7
B7
E7
To Coda
I wan - na be your man.
1.
2.
E7
A7
E7
B7
A7
E7
B7
D.S. al Coda

Coda
E7
I wan-na be your man,
I wan-na be your man,
A7
I wan-na be your man,
E7
I wan-na be your man,
I wan-na be your man,
B7
A7
E7
I wan-na be your man.

All My Loving

Words and Music by John Lennon and Paul McCartney

C♯m
A
B7
1.
E
N.C.
And I'll send all my lov-ing to you.
2. I'll pre-
2.
E
N.C.
C♯m
C aug
you.
All my lov-ing I will send to
E
C♯m
you,
All my lov-ing dar-
C aug
To Coda
E
N.C.
A
-ling, I'll be true.

E
B7
E
F♯m
B7
E
D.S. al Coda
N.C.
3. Close your
Coda
E
C♯m
All my lov - ing, all my lov - ing,
E
C♯m
oo all my lov - ing I will send to you.
E

She's a Woman

Words and Music by John Lennon and Paul McCartney

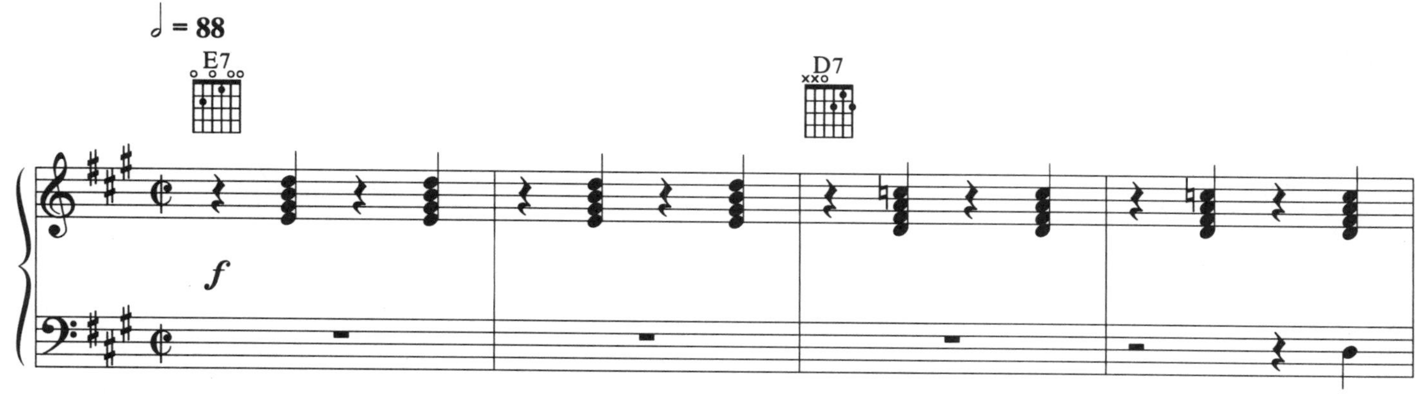

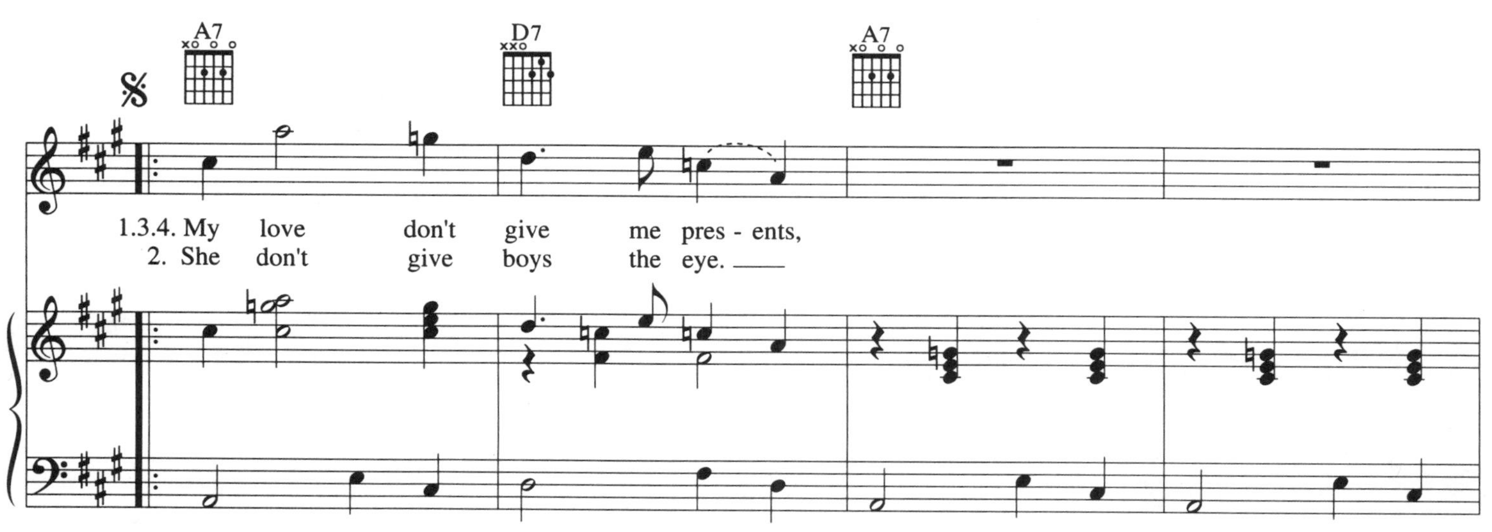

D7
A7
I know that she's no peas - ant.
She hates to see me cry.
D7
On - ly ev - er has to give me love for - ev - er and for - ev - er;
She is hap - py just to hear me say that I will nev - er leave her;
A7
D7
A7
My love don't give me pres - ents.
She don't give boys the eye.
E7
D7
Turn me on when I get lone - ly, Peo - ple tell me
She will nev - er make me jeal - ous, Gives me all her

A7
D7
A7
To Coda
that she's on - ly fool - in', I know she is - n't
time as well as lov - in', Don't ask me why.
1.
E7
2.
A7
C♯m
4 fr.
She's a wom - an who
F♯7
C♯m
4 fr.
D
E7
un - der - stands; She's a wom - an who loves her man.
3.
A7

D7
A7
E7
D7
A7
C#m
4 fr.
F#7
She's a wom - an who un - der - stands; __
C#m
4 fr.
D
E7
D.S. al Coda
She's a wom - an who loves her man. __
Coda
She's a wom -

A7
She's a wom - an.
D7
She's a wom - an.
She's a wom -
A7
an.
E7
She's a wom - an.
D7
A7
Repeat and Fade
She's a wom - an.
She's a wom -
- an.
- an.

Things We Said Today

Words and Music by John Lennon and Paul McCartney

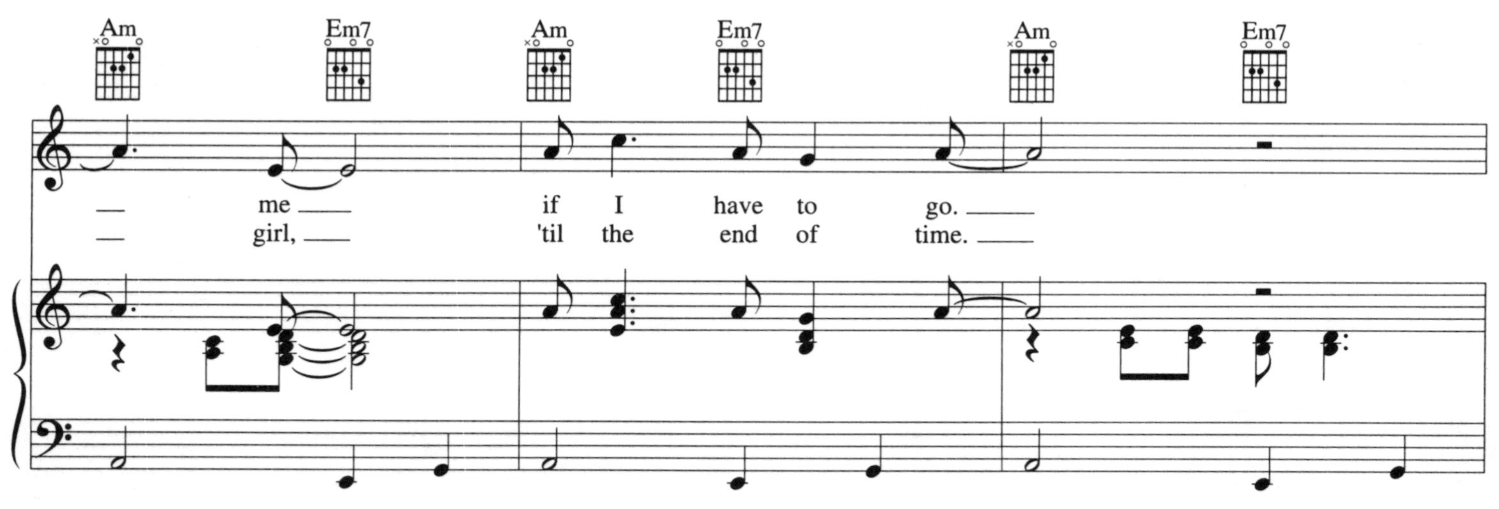

Am
C
C9
Some - day when I'm lone - ly
Some - day when we're dream - ing
F
B♭
Am
Em7
wish - ing you weren't so far a - way,
deep in love, not a lot to say,
Then I will re - mem -
Then we will re - mem -
Am
Em7
Am
Em7
1. Am
Em7
- ber Things we said to - day.
- ber Things we said to - day.
2. A
A
D7
Me, I'm just the luck - y kind,

B7
E7
A
Love to hear you say that love is love. And though we may
D7
B7
B♭
be blind, Love is here to stay and that's e - nough
Am
Em7
Am
Em7
Am
Em7
to make you mine, girl, Be the on - ly one.
Am
Em7
Am
Em7
Am
Em7
Love me all the time, girl,

Am
Em7
To Coda
Am
C
we'll go on and on.
Some - day when we're
C9
F
B♭
dream - ing, deep in love, not a lot to say;
Am
Em7
Am
Em7
Am
Em7
Then we will re - mem - ber things we said to - day.
A
D.S. al Coda
Coda
Repeat and Fade

I Feel Fine

Words and Music by John Lennon and Paul McCartney

♩ = 176

G7

1. Ba - by's good to me, you know, She's hap - py as can be,
2.3. Ba - by says she's mine, you know, She tells me all the time,

D

you know, she said so. I'm in love with her
you know, she said so. I'm in love with her

D♭

C
B♭
G7
G
— and I — feel — fine.
I'm so
— and I — feel — fine.
Bm
C
D
G
Bm
glad that she's my lit-tle girl. —
She's so glad she's
C
D
G7
tell-ing all — the world —
That her ba-by buys her things, — you know, — he
D
buys her dia-mond rings — you know, — she said so.

D♭
C
B♭
To Coda
G7
She's in love with me and I feel fine.
D7
D.C. al Coda
Coda
G7
fine.
D
D♭
C
B♭
She's in love with me and I feel
G7
N.C.
Repeat and Fade
fine.

Rickenbacker

Everybody's Trying to Be My Baby

Words and Music by Carl Lee Perkins

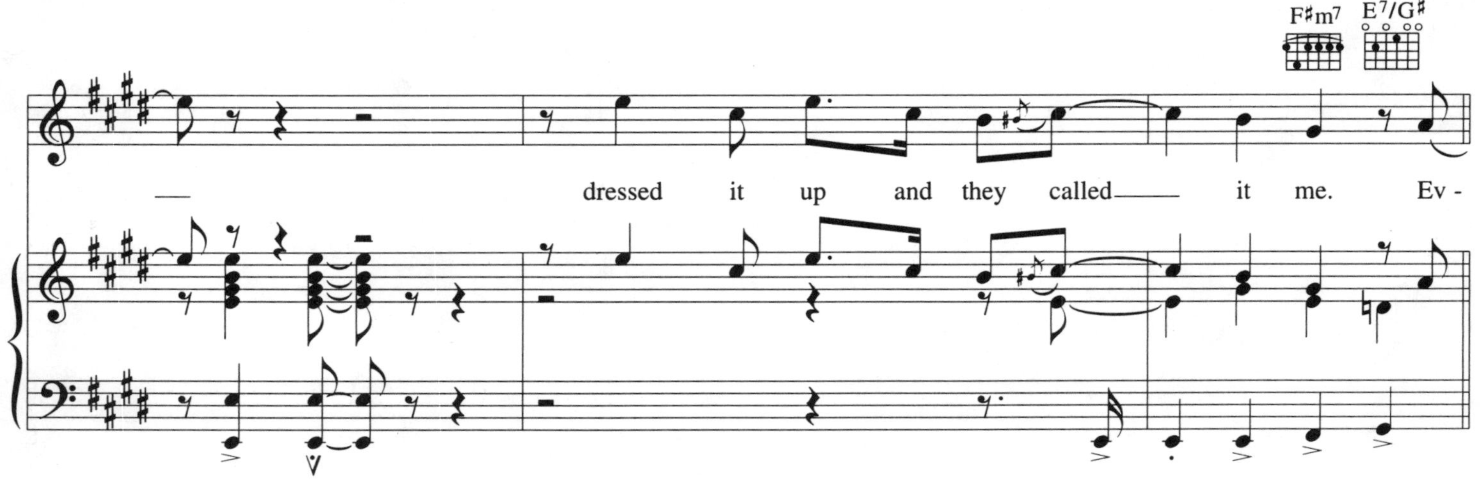

B7
A7
be my baby, ev - 'ry-bo-dy's tryin' to be my ba-by now.
1.
E
E
Woke up last night,
half past four,
fif - ty wo - men knock - in' on my door. Ev -
F♯m7
E7/G♯
3
2.
E
E7
(1st solo)

A7
E7
B7
A7
E
E
Went out last night, I
took some hon - ey
did - n't stay late,
'fore I got home I had a' nine - teen dates. Ev -
from a tree,
dressed it up and they called it me. Ev -
F♯m7
E7/G♯

A7
E
'ry - bo - dy's tryin' to be my ba - by, ev - 'ry - bo - dy's tryin' to
B7
A7
3º To Coda
be my ba - by, ev - 'ry - bo - dy's tryin' to be my ba - by now.
E
1. (Continue to 2nd solo)
2. (Back to 𝄋 and 2nd lyric)
2. Well they
E9(♯5)
(2nd solo)

A7
E7(♯9)
B7
A7
E
E7(♯9)
A9
fr6

E7
B7
A7
E
D.%. al Coda
(to 1st lyric)
Went
Coda
E
E dim
B7
E
E9
fr6

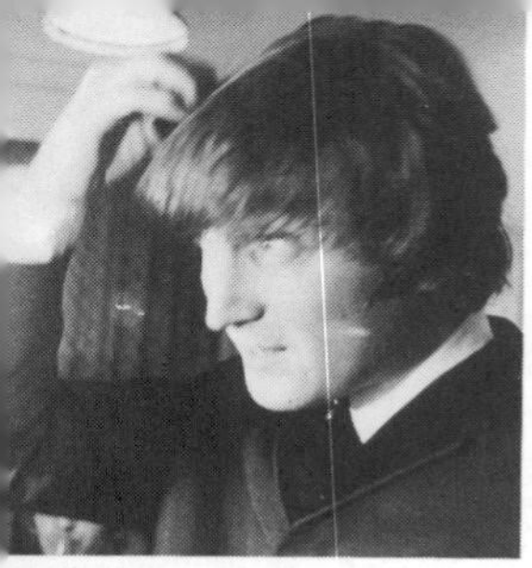

I'm a Loser

Words and Music by John Lennon and Paul McCartney

♩ = 176

Am7 D7 Am7

I'm a los - - - - - er, I'm a los - - - - -

D7 Am7 F D7

- er, And I'm not what I ap - pear ___ to be. ___

𝄋 G D F

1. Of all the love ___ I have won ___ or have lost ___
2. Al - though I laugh ___ and I act ___ like a clown; ___
3. What have I done ___ to de - serve ___ such a fate, ___

G D F

— There is one love ___ I should nev - er have crossed. _
— Be - neath this mask ___ I am wear - ing a frown. _
— I re - a - lize ___ I have left it too late. ___

G
D
She was a girl in a mil-
My tears are fal - - - - ling like rain
And so it's true pride comes be-
F
G
- lion, my friend.
from the sky.
- fore a fall.
I should have known
Is it for her
I'm tel - ling you
D
F
G
she would win in the end;
or my - self that I cry?
so that you won't lose all.
I'm a los -
Am7
D7
Am7
- er,
And I lost
some - one who's near

D7
G
Em
— to me. I'm a los - - - - - - - er, And I'm
Am7
1.
F
D7
2,3.
F
D7
G
not what I ap-pear — to be. — — to be. —
D
F
G
D
F
G
Am7
D7
Am7
D7
G
Em
Am7
F
D7
D.S. to Fade

Dizzy Miss Lizzy

Words and Music by Larry Williams

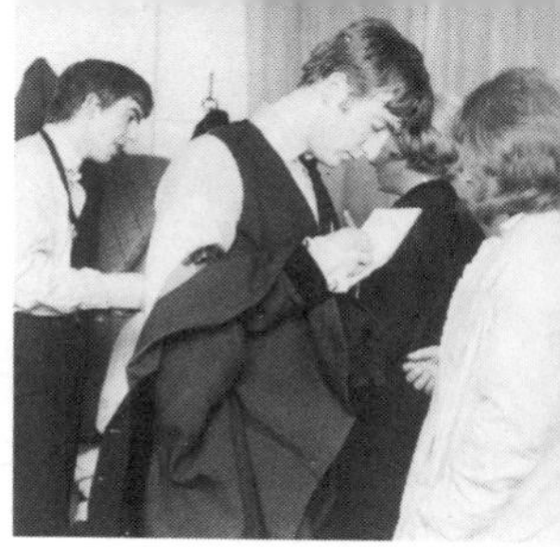

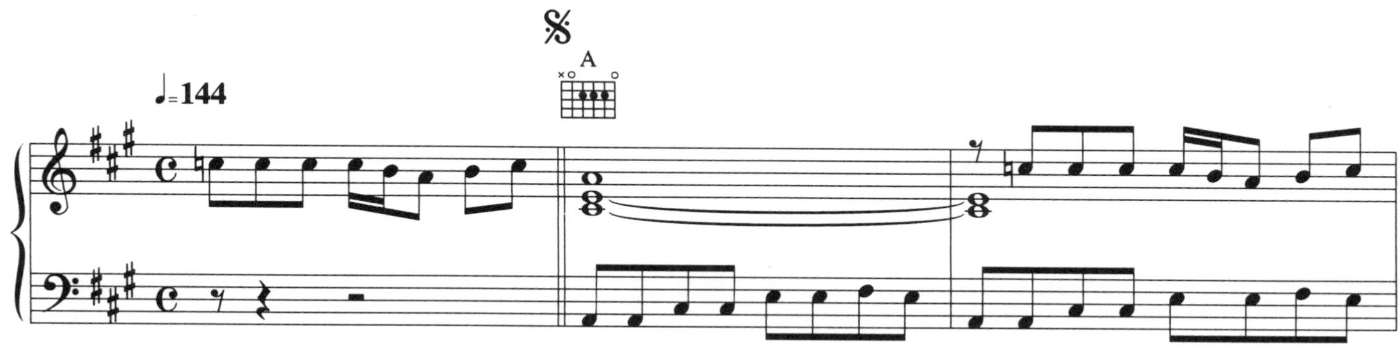

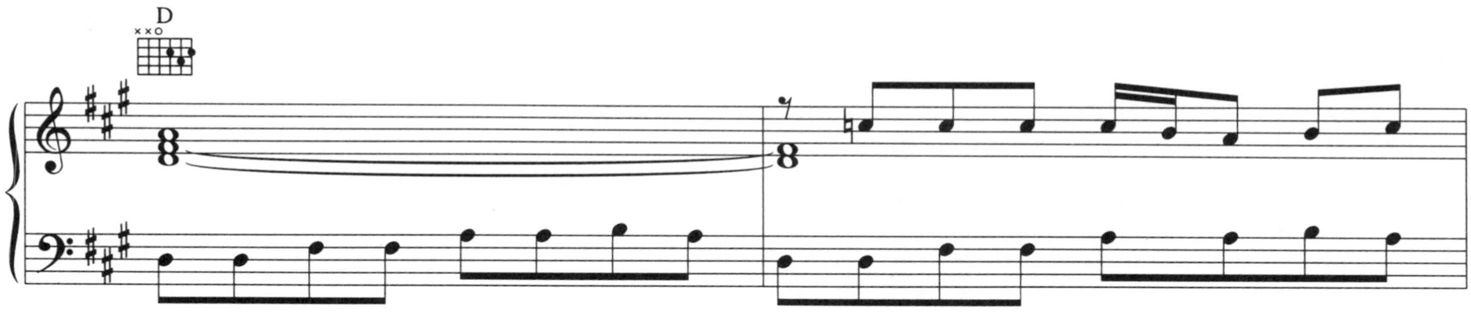

D
A
E
1. You make me diz - zy Miss
A
Liz - zy the way you rock 'n' roll,
(Verses 2, 3, 4 & 5 see block lyric)
D
you make me diz - zy Miss Liz - zy when we do the stroll.
A
Come on come on come on come on

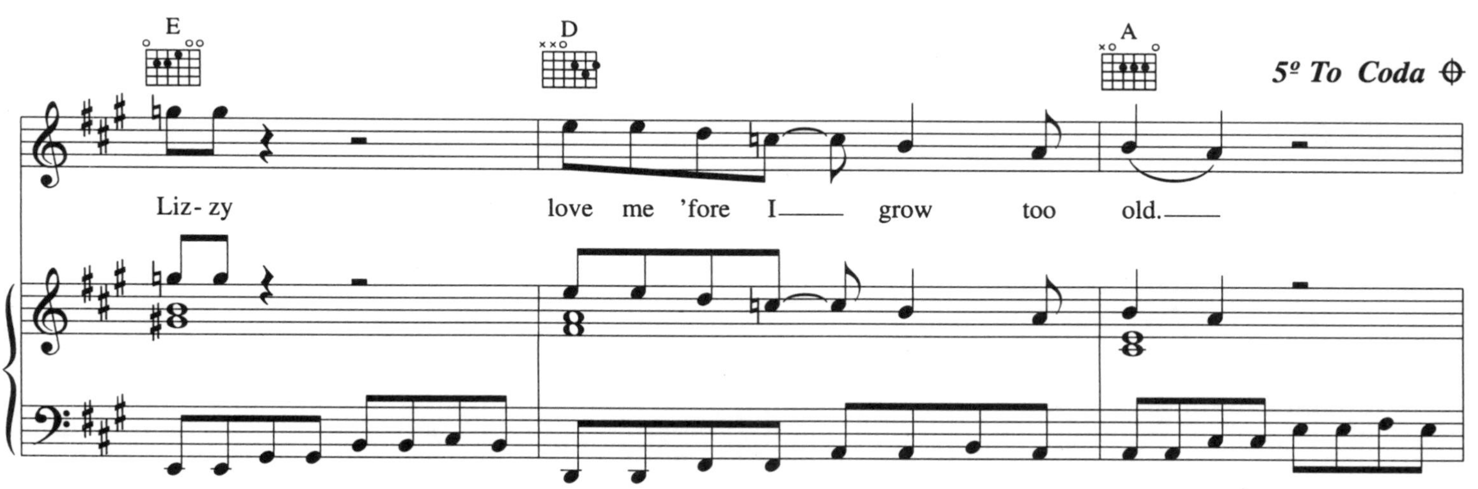

Verse 2:
Come on, give me fever,
Put your little hand in mine
Just make me dizzy Miss Lizzy
Who cares, you look so fine
You're just a rockin' and a rollin'
Girl, I said I wish you were mine.

Verse 3:
You make me dizzy Miss Lizzy
When you call my name
Ooh baby,
Say you're driving me insane
Come on come on come on Lizzy
I want to be your lovin' man.

Verse 4:
Come on, give me fever,
Put your little hand in mine
Just make me dizzy Miss Lizzy
Girl, you look so fine
You're just a rockin' and a rollin'
Girl, I said I wish you were mine.

Verse 5:
You make me dizzy Miss Lizzy
When you call my name, girl
Ooh baby,
Say you're driving me insane
Come on come on come on Lizzy
I want to be your lovin' man.

Rock and Roll Music

Words and Music by Chuck Berry

♩=162

A7 A7

Just let me hear some of that rock and roll mu - sic, (1, 2, 3.) a - (4.) a -

D7

- ny old way you choose - it; / - ny old time you use — it; it's got a back beat, you can't lose — it, a -

A7 E7

- ny old time you use — it. Got - ta be rock and roll mu - sic, If —

ff

4º To Coda ⊕
A
E7
A
N.C.
I got no kick a-gainst
you wan-na dance with me, if you wan-na dance with me. I took my loved one ov-er
Way down south they had a
E7
A
mo-dern jazz, un-less they try to play it too darn fast,
'cross the tracks and she can hear a man a-wail-in' sax,
ju-bi-lee, them Geor-gia folks, they had a jam-bo-ree,
D
and lose the beau-ty of the me-lo-dy, un-til they sound just like a
I must ad-mit they had a rock-in' band, and they were blow-in' like a
they're drink-in' home brew from a wood-en cup, the folks were danc-in' there got
E
3º D.S. al Coda
⊕ Coda
A
sym-pho-ny. That's why I go for that
hur-ri-can'. And start-ed play-in' that
all shook up. And start-ed play-in' that

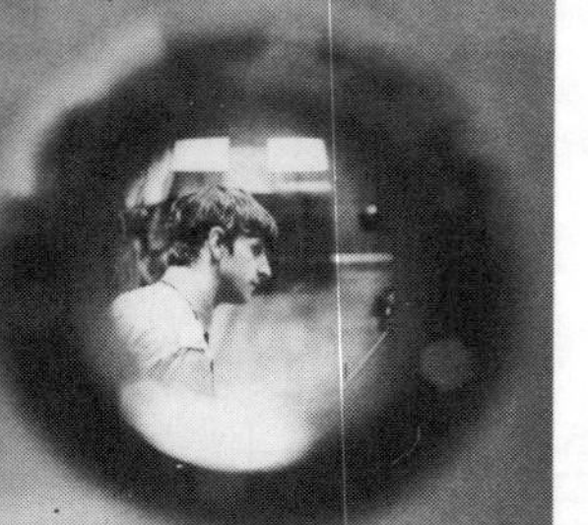

Ticket to Ride

Words and Music by John Lennon and Paul McCartney

E7
F♯m
D7
F♯m
She's got a tick-et to ride,
She's got a tick-et to ri-
G
F♯m
E7
-hi-hide,
She's got a tick-et to ride,
but she don't care.
1. A
2. A
2. She
I
D7
don't know why she's rid-in' so high,
She ought to

E
D7
think right; She ought to do right by me.
Be - fore she gets to say - ing good - bye
She ought to think twice, She ought to do right by
E
A
me.
1. I think I'm gon - na be sad.
2. She said that liv - ing with me
I think it's to - day, yeh! The
is bring - ing her down, yeh! For

Bm7
girl that's driv - ing me mad is go - ing a - way. Yeh!
she would nev - er be free when I was a - round. Yeh!
E7
F♯m
D7
F♯m
Oh, She's got a tick - et to ride, She's got a tick - et to ri -
G
F♯m
E7
1. A
hi - hide, She's got a tick - et to ride, but she don't care.
2. A
Repeat and Fade
I My ba - by don't care.

Matchbox

Words and Music by Carl Lee Perkins

♩=156

N.C.

A

I said I'm sit-tin' here___ watch - in', match-box hole in my clothes;_

D7

I said I'm sit-tin' here watch - in',

A

match - box hole in my clothes. I

E7
D7
To Coda
A
ain't got no match - es, but I sure got a long — way to go. —
E7
A
I'm an ol' — poor boy and I — ain't — got a home;
D7
— I'm an ol' — poor boy and I'm a long — way from home; —
A
E7
D7
— and ev - 'ry - thing I do, turns out — might - y

A
E7
A
wrong.
Guitar solo
D7
A
E7
D7
1.
2.
A
E7
E7
Well if you don't

A
want my peach - es ho - ney, please don't shake my tree;
D7
if you don't want a - ny of those peach - es ho - ney, please don't mess a - round my tree.
A
E7
D7
I got news for you, ba - by, leave me here in mi - se - ry.
D.%. al Coda
Coda
A
E7
Well, I said I'm
A
A6

Honey Don't

Words and Music by Carl Lee Perkins

♩=180

N.C. — E

E

1. Well, how come you say you will — when you won't?
(Verses 2 & 3 see block lyric)

C — E

Say you do, ba - by, when you don't? — Let me know, ho - ney,

C

how you feel; — tell the truth now, is love real? — But ah -

B13
B11
E
-hah, well, ho-ney don't.
Well, ho-ney, don't,
E
ho-ney, don't,
A7
ho-ney, don't,
ho-ney, don't.
E
B7
Say you will when you won't, ah-

1.
A7
To Coda
E
- hah, ho - ney, don't.
Well, I love
2, 3.
E
E
C
E
C
B7
E

Verse 2:
Well I love you baby and I want you to know
I like the way that you wear your clothes
Everything about you is so doggone sweet
You got that sand all over your feet
But ah ha, honey don't.

Verse 3:
Well I love you baby on a Saturday night
Sunday morning you don't look right
You've been out painting the town
Ah ah honey been steppin' around
But ah ha, honey don't.

Kansas City/Hey Hey Hey Hey

Kansas City: Words and Music by Jerry Leiber and Mike Stoller

Hey Hey Hey Hey: Words and Music by Richard Penniman

♩=134

G C7

ff

G C7 C♯7 D7

Ah, ___

G7 C/G G7 C/G G7 C/G G7 C/G

3º instrumental

___ Kan - sas Ci - ty, gon - na get my ba - by back home ___
___ Kan - sas Ci - ty, gon - na get my ba - by one time ___

G7 C/G G7 C/G G7 C/G G7 C/G C7 F/C C7 F/C

___ a yeah, yeah, ___ I'm goin' ___ to Kan - sas Ci - ty,
___ yeah, yeah, ___ I'm goin' ___ to Kan - sas Ci - ty,

C7 F/C C7 F/C G7 C/G G7 C/G
gon - na get my ba - by back home,
gon - na get my ba - by one time,
a yeah, yeah.
a yeah, yeah.
G7 C/G G7 D7 G/D D7 G/D
Well it's a long, long time since
It's just a one, two, three, four,
C7 F/C C7 F/C G7 C/G G7 C/G
1, 2.
G C7 C♯7 D7
my ba - by's been gone.
five, six, se - ven, eight, nine.
Ah,
3.
G G7 C/G G7 C/G G7 C/G G7 C/G
Segue 'Hey Hey Hey'
1, 2. Hey hey hey hey,
hey ba -
3, 4. Bye bye, bye bye, bye bye,

G7 C/G G7 C/G G7 C/G G7 C/G C7 F/C C7 F/C
- by, ooh, now child,
bye bye, bye bye, bye bye, so long, so long,
C7 F/C C7 F/C G7 C/G G7 C/G G7 C/G G7 C/G
I said a' yeah now child. Oh now tell me ba -
so long, bye bye, bye bye, bye bye,
D7 G/D D7 G/D C7 F/C C7 F/C
1, 2, 3.
G7 C/G G7 C/G
- by what's been wrong with you.
bye bye ba - by bye bye.
D7
4.
G/B C C♯dim D7 G G9
fr3
fr4
Hey hey hey bye.
3
3

Love Me Do

Words and Music by John Lennon and Paul McCartney

♩ = 142

G7 Csus2 G7 Csus2

G7 Csus2 G

G Csus2 G Csus2

Love, love me do, you know I love you, I'll

G Csus2 C N.C.

al - ways be true, so please Love me

G7
Csus2
G7
1. Csus2
do. ___ Woh, ___ love ___ me do. ___
2. Csus2
D
C
Some - one to love, Some - bod - y
(2° Instr.)
G
D
C
G
To Coda
D.S. al Coda
N.C.
new. ___ Some - one to love, Some - one like you.
Coda
G